HISTORY'S GREATEST WARRIORS

Vikings

by Peter Anderson

BELLWETHER MEDIA · MINNEAPOLIS, MN

Are you ready to take it to the extreme?
Torque books thrust you into the action-packed world
of sports, vehicles, mystery, and adventure. These books
may include dirt, smoke, fire, and dangerous stunts.
Warning: read at your own risk.

Library of Congress Cataloging-in-Publication Data

Anderson, Peter, 1965-
 Vikings / by Peter Anderson.
     p. cm. -- (Torque: history's greatest warriors)
 Summary: "Engaging images accompany information about vikings. The combination of high-interest
subject matter and light text is intended for students in grades 3 through 7"--Provided by publisher.
 Includes bibliographical references and index.
 ISBN 978-1-60014-632-9 (hardcover : alk. paper)
 1. Vikings--Warfare--Juvenile literature. I. Title.
 DL66.A53 2012
 948'.022--dc22   2011003053

This edition first published in 2012 by Bellwether Media, Inc.

Printed in the United States of America, North Mankato, MN.

080111   1187

Contents

Who Were the Vikings?

For over 300 years during the **Dark Ages**, Vikings brought terror to northern Europe. The sight of Viking **longships** made people flee for their lives. The Vikings would **raid**, burn, and **pillage** the towns and villages of their enemies. No one was safe.

Vikings were deadly warriors. They were also skilled shipbuilders, sailors, and explorers. Their journeys took them east to Asia and west to North America. They set up **colonies** and **trade routes** in many places.

Viking Fact

The Vikings were also called *Norsemen*, which means "people of the north."

The Vikings came from **Scandinavia**. This region of northern Europe includes the lands of Denmark, Norway, Sweden, and Finland. They sailed from these lands to attack other parts of Europe.

Vikings were **pagans**. They would often pillage Christian churches. The churches were poorly defended. Vikings could easily steal their gold and other riches.

Viking Fact

The Vikings were the first Europeans to reach North America. Leif Eriksson and his men landed there around 1000 CE. That is almost 500 years before Christopher Columbus!

SCANDINAVIA

EUROPE

Berserkers were the deadliest Viking warriors. They fought in a furious rage and did not care about their own safety. Even their friends were not safe. Berserkers behaved like wild animals. Some wore wolf skins over their backs and heads. Meeting a berserker in battle usually meant death.

Valhalla: Great Hall of Heroes

Vikings believed that brave warriors who died on the battlefield would go to Valhalla. This great hall was ruled by Odin, king of the Norse gods. The heroes would fight every day. Their wounds would heal at night and they would feast together. This would go on until Ragnarök, the death and rebirth of the Norse world.

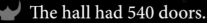 The hall had 540 doors.

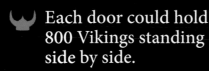 Each door could hold 800 Vikings standing side by side.

The roof was made of golden shields.

The rafters were large spears.

Viking Training

Viking children learned how to fight from an early age. They practiced with swords, bows and arrows, and other weapons. Both boys and girls could become warriors. They joined raids when they were skilled enough to fight well.

Vikings also learned how to sail. They were taught how to read maps and **navigate**. It was important for Vikings to know ocean **tides** and **currents** so they could plan the best routes.

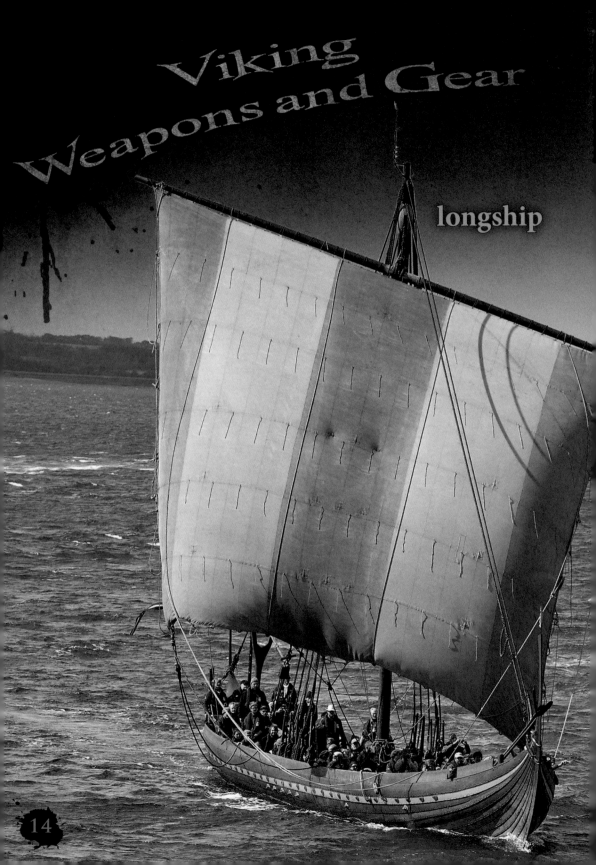

Viking
Weapons and Gear

longship

Vikings used longships to navigate the sea. These ships were narrow with a shallow **draft**.

Longships had sails and oars. The Vikings used sails to move on the open sea. Oars helped them move fast in shallow water. They could also give ships a burst of speed at sea.

Viking Fact

Each longship could carry more than 50 Vikings. Ships often traveled together in fleets.

sword

battle-axe

bow and arrow

The Vikings fought with many weapons. Most warriors used spears. Some Vikings had swords or battle-axes. Bows and arrows were used to attack enemies from a distance. Vikings often used flaming arrows to set entire villages on fire!

Vikings also needed protection from enemy weapons. Most wore leather helmets and armor to protect their heads and bodies. Some Vikings had iron helmets and **chain mail** armor. Wooden shields were used to block enemy attacks.

The Decline of the Vikings

The Dark Ages were a bloody and destructive time. Few people could stand up to the Vikings. That began to change in the late 1000s. England and France became more powerful. They were able to fight back against the Vikings with better weapons and ships. They were even brave enough to attack the Vikings.

Norway and Denmark also became less warlike. The Vikings went on fewer raids. Many Scandinavian people **converted** from their pagan beliefs to Christianity. Over time, they stopped raiding and pillaging. The Viking Age soon came to an end. The once fierce Vikings were no more.

Glossary

berserkers—Vikings who fought in a wild rage

chain mail—armor made from woven links of metal

colonies—territories owned and settled by people from another country

converted—changed beliefs

currents—movements of the sea

Dark Ages—the time from about 500 CE to 1000 CE; the Vikings were most powerful during the Dark Ages.

draft—how deep the bottom of a ship goes beneath the water's surface

longships—long, narrow ships; a Viking longship used a sail and oars to move.

navigate—to find one's way in an unfamiliar place

pagans—people who believe in many gods

pillage—to violently steal valuables from a place

raid—to attack suddenly

Scandinavia—a region in northern Europe; Scandinavia includes Norway, Sweden, Denmark, Finland, and many islands.

tides—the rises and falls of the sea; tides are caused by the Moon's gravity pulling on the water.

trade routes—paths taken by people to transport goods

To Learn More

AT THE LIBRARY

Doeden, Matt. *Weapons of the Vikings.*
Mankato, Minn.: Capstone Press, 2009.

Hinds, Kathryn. *Vikings: Masters of the Sea.*
New York, N.Y.: Marshall Cavendish Benchmark, 2010.

Hynson, Colin. *How People Lived in Viking Times.* New York,
N.Y.: The Rosen Pub. Group's PowerKids Press, 2009.

ON THE WEB

Learning more about Vikings
is as easy as 1, 2, 3.

1. Go to www.factsurfer.com.

2. Enter "Vikings" into the search box.

3. Click the "Surf" button and you will see a list
of related Web sites.

With factsurfer.com, finding more information
is just a click away.

WWW.FACTSURFER.COM

Index